Fifteen Lakes and Trails of Central Idaho

A selected guide for hikers,
mountain bicyclists, and cross-country skiers.

by Michael LaFortune
Humorous Illustrations by Mark Larson

— A Maverick Publication —

Copyright © 1990 Michael LaFortune

Maverick Publications
Drawer 5007 • Bend, OR 97708

This book is dedicated to those who find splendor and solace in nature's universal design.

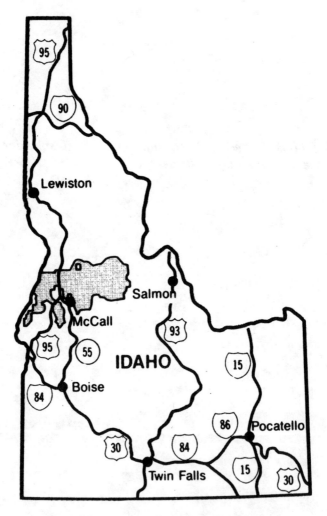

Vicinity map showing the Payette National Forest.

Contents

Introduction

The lakes and trails of Central Idaho have some of the most scenic alpine terrain to be found in the state. A large variety of wildflowers exist along with an abundance of trout stocked in the remote mountain lakes. Rugged granite peaks and deep glacial formed valleys support a large mixture of wildlife. It is not uncommon to see deer and elk grazing on near-by mountainsides with periodic sightings of bear, moose and beaver on some of the more secluded trails.

History and legends surround these mountains and lakes. From the first Indians that fished for salmon along the banks of the Payette River to the Finnish settlers who traveled by horse and wagon into Long Valley. The legend of Polly Bemis and the arduous Chinese miners who built placer mines throughout the hills. The emergency landing of an Army Airforce bomber in 1943. The German immigrant, Fred Burgdorf and his hot springs resort along with the many Olympic contenders that have skied and jumped for gold at the Payette Lakes Little Ski Hill, all share a part of Central Idaho's past.

Preceding each trail is a list of five important facts. The trails are listed as a day hike or backpack. A day hike is usually very short in distance or one which lacks suitable sites for camping. Trails listed as backpack have campsites available for an overnight stay and are longer in distance to travel. Combine you may prefer to spend the night because of its scenic beauty, difficulty of the hike or size of fish caught. Mountain bikes and cross-country ski trails are one day trips. Some of the ski trails at Ponderosa State Park and The Little Ski Hill will take less time depending on your ability.

Distance one direction is from the trailhead or closest point accessible by car.

Elevation gain is the total footage accumulated. Any significant elevation loss is also shown.

Approximate travel time is from the basic rate of two miles per hour with allowances for rest stops, steepness of the trail and elevation gain.

The trails' highest and lowest elevation along with the distance in miles are shown in the graphs.

The United States Geological Survey (U.S.G.S.) topographic map's name and date is also included. It is highly recommended when venturing out into an unknown region that you pick one up showing the area in which you are hiking, riding or skiing. A hardware or outdoor store usually has them in stock. They are inexpensive and easy to read.

The topographic map at the bottom of the page is either enlarged or reduced in size. Areas that are unshaded

represent little or no vegetation. The figures at the lakes and peaks are elevation marks above sea level. All maps are north oriented. The trails are clearly marked in bold lines so as not to be confused with other trail crossings. Campsites are not shown on the map but are included in the text.

It is always very important to carry your own water or take a water purification system with you. The threat of Giardia and other intestinal viruses is prevalent in all lakes and streams no matter how clear or clean they may appear to be. If water is available from a government well, it will also be noted.

A Payette National Forest map showing roads and trails can be obtained at the District Ranger's Office in McCall. For a last minute source of trail information, talk to a ranger. They can often tell you about any trail closures and conditions in the forest. Most of the trails listed are open from May through October. Cross-country ski trails are usually open from November through March. Be prepared for weather changes even in July since it has been known to snow in the higher elevations around McCall. Due to natural causes, trail conditions can change at any moment. Those on mountain bikes should ride at a safe and courteous speed using extreme caution at all times.

By enjoying these lakes and trails, you are accepting an obligation to both the delicate conformation of the forest and to those who will follow in the years to come. Therefore by your admission, you should leave the area unaltered. By adhering to this ethic, it is believed that the least amount of damage to the environment and the least offense to your fellow outdoorsmen will occur.

—The Author

Boulder Lake Trailhead

BOULDER LAKE ROAD

SECTION 1.

Louie Lake Trail
Day hike or backpack
Mountain bike
Cross-country ski

Boulder Lake Trail
Day hike or backpack

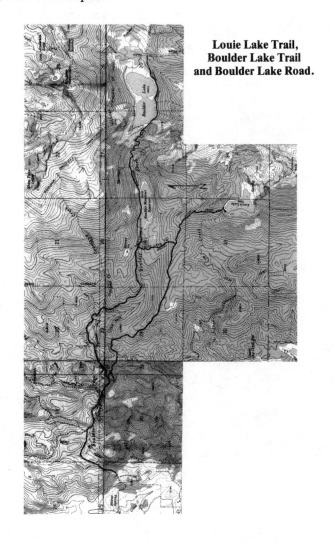

**Louie Lake Trail,
Boulder Lake Trail
and Boulder Lake Road.**

BOULDER LAKE ROAD

In 1848, the discovery of gold in California saw men and boys from around the world in search of the precious mineral. When vast amounts of ore deposits had been depleted, they traveled north, in quest of greater riches. During the 1860s, roads were built following trails used by the Indians who had hunted and fished in the area. Irish, German and Chinese immigrants began staking their claims along creeks and valleys. Poorman Creek, which you will cross on the way to Boulder Meadows Reservoir, had a Post Office at the entrance to the mine. A ditch, hand dug by the Chinese to move water around the mountain, is still being used today and is the oldest one on record in the Payette National Forest.

By the early 1880s, the Finnish settled in Long Valley to farm the rich and fertile soil. Clarence Shaw traveled by mule team from Kansas in 1889 and raised nine kids on the

Boulder Lake

Boulder Lake

160-acre homestead at the base of Boulder Mountain. Boulder Lake Road was part of a 30-mile pack trail that lead to the south fork of the Salmon River. It was used mostly by government trappers, packers and the Forest Service to fight fires in the area.

In 1925, Clarence Shaw and his son, Roy, hauled cement by horse and mule to Shaw Twins Lake and formed a dam to increase the water supply for irrigation on the now 720-acre ranch. Roy was also the first one to plant trout in the high mountain lakes. Using milkcans and a packstring, he hauled the fingerlings from a fish hatchery in Cascade to the waiting lakes in the area.

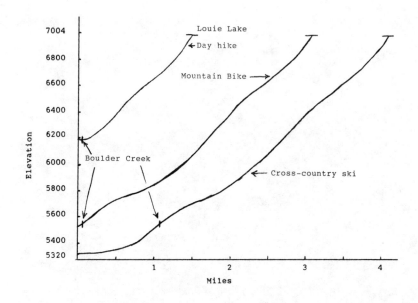

Louie Lake Trail

LOUIE LAKE TRAIL
Day hike or backpack
Mountain bike
Cross-country ski

Day hike or backpack
Distance one direction: 1.5 miles
Elevation gain: 804 feet
Approximate travel time: 1 hour, 30 minutes
Topographic map: U.S.G.S. Paddy Flat 1973

The first mile of the Louie Lake Trail takes you through tall spindly Tamarack and mature Ponderosa pine before intersecting with the old jeep trail. The next mile climbs steadily along a ridge with several scenic viewpoints of Long Valley. Upon reaching Louie Lake, the rugged sheer cliff of 8,052-foot Jughandle Mountain watches over the alpine lake framed with young aspens. A short distance to the right is the hand-hewn remains of an old log cabin that the Finnish once lived in while hauling dirt to build the earthen dam.

Heading south from McCall on Highway 55, turn left at Farm to Market and follow for 3.5 miles to Boulder Lake Road No. 403. The pavement ends in one mile at a cattle guard. Follow the dirt road for 3 miles to Louie Lake Trail on your right. (A half mile before the end of the road.)

LOUIE LAKE TRAIL
Mountain bike
Half day ride round trip
Distance one direction: 3 miles
Elevation gain: 1,524 feet
Topographic map: U.S.G.S. Paddy Flat 1973

Follow Farm to Market Road for 3.5 miles to Boulder Lake Road (No. 403). Take Boulder Lake Road for 2.4 miles to an old jeep road on your right (No. 445). It is best to park here and cross the creek. The road does get steep and narrow in the first mile as you ride through thick stands of alder. Continue straight at the first logging road. Stay to the left at the next two crossroads. At 2 miles is the hiking trail on the left. The road is steep with large rocks and washouts making for a challenging ride. With this in mind, extreme caution should be used when returning.

LOUIE LAKE TRAIL
Cross-country ski
One day ski round trip
Distance one direction: 4 miles
Elevation gain: 1,684 feet
Approximate travel time: 2 hours 30 minutes
Topographic maps: Paddy Flat 1973; Lake Fork 1973;
McCall 1973

Jughandle Mountain with Louie Lake in the foreground.

A half mile south of McCall is Farm to Market Road. Turn left and follow for 3.5 miles to Boulder Lake Road. During the winter, this road is only plowed out for the next mile to the top of the hill where the pavement ends. Continue on skis for 2 miles to the old Louie Lake jeep trail on the right. For off-track cross-country skiing, the trail to Louie Lake offers a variety of terrain. This backcountry ski trail is steep with a thick crop of trees and rocks. For a more gentle ski, continue along Boulder Lake Road.

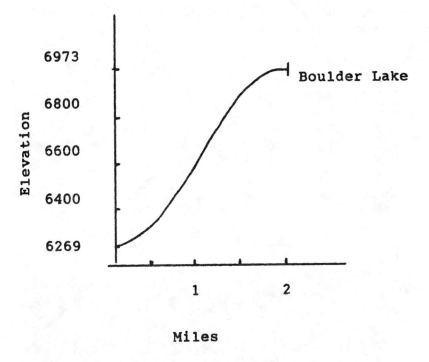

Boulder Lake Trail: One day trip or backpack

BOULDER LAKE TRAIL
Day hike or backpack
Distance one direction: 2 miles
Elevation gain: 704 feet
Approximate travel time: 1 hour
Topographic map: U.S.G.S. Paddy Flat 1973

Boulder Lake Trail is well-maintained and easily accessible for an afternoon hike or overnight stay. Fishermen will want to try their luck at Boulder Lake, which is stocked with pan-sized trout in the early spring.

Take Farm to Market Road (a ½ mile south of McCall on the left), for 3.5 miles to Boulder Lake Road No. 403. Follow Boulder Lake Road for 4 miles to Boulder Meadows Reservoir. This is the end of the road. Parking and campsites are located below the earth dam. The trail starts to the left, looking east, at the edge of the reservoir. For the next 2¼ mile, hike along the rocky bank before gradually climbing through dense undergrowth of bracken and alder. Just before reaching the lake is a series of short switchbacks. At Boulder Lake is a dike of granite and cement carefully placed for irrigation. The trail crosses Boulder Creek and follows the lake for a ½ mile through campsites surrounded by large, towering spruce and fir.

Trail around Boulder Lake

PONDEROSA STATE PARK

SECTION 2.
Day hike
Mountain bike
Cross-country ski

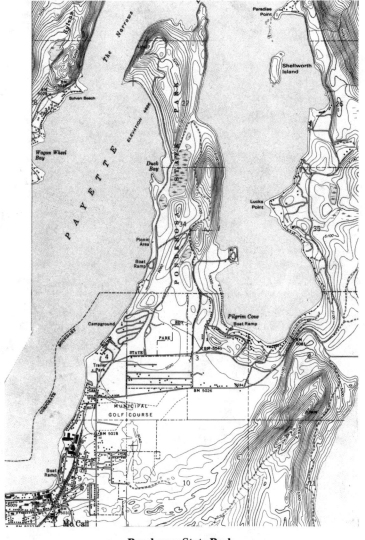

Ponderosa State Park

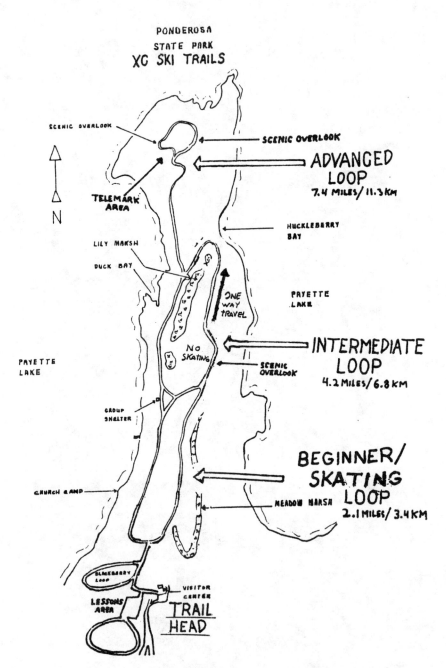

Ponderosa State Park: Cross-country ski trails

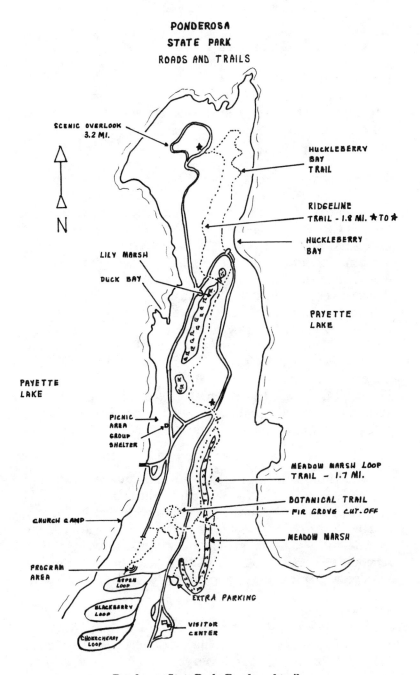

PONDEROSA
STATE PARK
ROADS AND TRAILS

SCENIC OVERLOOK
3.2 MI.

N

HUCKLEBERRY
BAY
TRAIL

RIDGELINE
TRAIL - 1.8 MI. ★ TO ★

HUCKLEBERRY
BAY

LILY MARSH

DUCK BAY

PAYETTE
LAKE

PAYETTE
LAKE

PICNIC
AREA
GROUP
SHELTER

MEADOW MARSH LOOP
TRAIL - 1.7 MI.

BOTANICAL TRAIL
FIR GROVE CUT-OFF

CHURCH CAMP

MEADOW MARSH

PROGRAM
AREA

ASPEN
LOOP

EXTRA PARKING

BLACKBERRY
LOOP

VISITOR
CENTER

CHOKECHERRY
LOOP

Ponderosa State Park: Roads and trails

23

PONDEROSA STATE PARK
Day hike
Mountain bike
Cross-country ski
*A day-use and overnight fee is charged. Campground reservations can be made no less than 10 days before arrival.

Ponderosa State park is located on a forested peninsula two miles northeast of McCall city center. Follow the signs from the corner of Highway 55 and Lake Street past the McCall City Golf Course. This 900-acre State Park has 170 campsites, picnicking, swimming, a deep draft boat launch, campfire programs and nature trails. During the winter, over 7 miles of well-groomed cross-country ski trails await the beginner through advanced nordic skier.

Since the early 1900s, the park has been preserved with the help of concerned citizens and government agencies. In 1965, this point of land became a State Park. Some of the old growth Ponderosa pine, also known as "Yellow Pine," are over 400 years old and reach heights of up to 150 feet or more with a diameter of up to 6 feet. Through natural succession in the coniferous forest, the faster growing Douglas fir will eventually become the dominant species.

Day hike:
Ponderosa Park has a botanical trail and several nature trails that wind along basaltic cliffs, through dense woods into meadows and marshes. Deer, fox, geese, beaver, osprey and eagle can occasionally be seen. Check with a park ranger for details on guided nature hikes and regularly scheduled evening programs. Drinking water and showers are also available at the campground.

Mountain bicyclist:
Mountain bicyclists will enjoy the 7.5-mile loop ride from the visitors' center to the scenic overlook of Payette Lake. All posted speed limits should be observed and caution should be used on the well-graveled roads. Due to the

delicate ecology within the park, no bicycles are allowed on any of the trails.

Cross-country ski:

During the winter months, Ponderosa Park offers several miles of double-track, machine-groomed ski trails. Those new at the sport, young and old, will want to try the first 2.1 mile/3.4 km beginner loop. This loop has some small hills, a downhill section and a 12-ft. skating lane. A lessons area is groomed from mid-January through March next to the visitors' center.

Advanced beginners and intermediate skiers will want to try the 4.2 mile/6.8 km intermediate ski loop. No skating is allowed along this trail. At 1.2 miles, a short climb off the track offers a picturesque view of the east arm of Payette Lake.

The 7.4 mile/11.3 km loop is more challenging and has several small telemark slopes at the north end of the park peninsula. This trail climbs towards a breath-taking scenic overlook of Payette Lake along a volcanic ridge that geologists say once crossed the lake.

The visitors' center at the trailhead is open on weekends and the park closes at 10 p.m. A use fee is charged at the self-collection pay station. Park-and-Ski stickers are not valid at Ponderosa Park although an Idaho State Park Passport can be purchased for one calendar year and is good at any Idaho State park. For more information contact:

Ponderosa State Park
P.O. Box A
McCall, ID 83638
(208) 634-2164

LICK CREEK ROAD

SECTION 3.

BOX LAKE TRAIL
Day hike or backpack

DUCK LAKE
Day hike

DUCK LAKE LOOKOUT

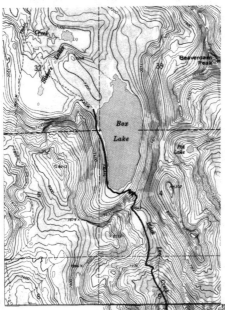

Box Lake Trail

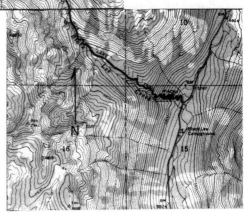

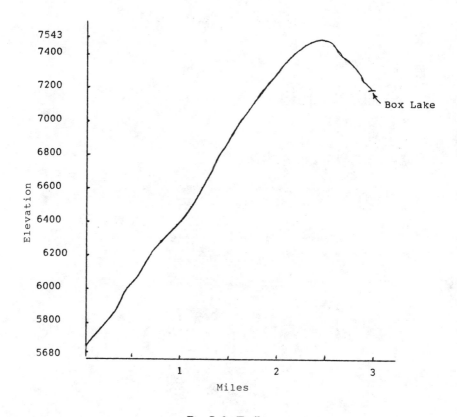

Box Lake Trail

BOX LAKE TRAIL
Day hike or backpack
Distance one direction: 3 miles
Elevation gain: 1,863 feet
Elevation loss: 343 feet
Approximate travel time: 3 hours
Topographic map: Fitsum Summit 1973, Box Lake 1979

Box Lake is one of the largest high-country lakes in the 2.3-million-acre Payette National Forest. Due to the steepness of the trail, it is not recommended for small children.

From the McCall Golf Course, turn right and follow

Box Lake

Lake Shore Drive for 2 miles to Lick Creek Road. The first mile of the gravel road follows little Payette Lake. Originally 485 acres, a small dam was built by the Lake Fork Irrigation District in 1926, increasing the size of the lake to 1,450 acres. In 1987, Little Payette Lake was chosen by the Idaho Department of Fish and Game as a trophy fish hatcher. The lake is currently stocked with Kamloops trout and selected strains of fingerlings with certain size, bait, and limit restrictions. Be sure to check with Idaho Fish and Game regulations concerning this lake.

At the east end of Little Payette Lake, Lick Creek Road and Lake Fork Creek meet in between a fortress of large granite boulders. In the early 1940s, a small power plant on this stream provided McCall with electricity. On Monday and Tuesday when wash was being done, an auxiliary gas generator was turned on for extra power.

At 6 miles is Lake Fork Campground where drinking water is available. Eleven miles on Lick Creek Road is Box

Lake Trail on the left. The first ½ mile is steep, with many switchbacks as you climb along Black Lee Creek. The trail crosses the creek at one mile, with more switchbacks, climbing gradually through stands of spruce and fir before reaching a large meadow. At the northwest end of this clearing is a small saddle overlooking Box Lake. The trail then drops down to the lake through several campsites. To the right, talus slopes from Beaverdam Peak reach out towards the lake. The trail continues around the lake into several other smaller lakes in the area.

Viewpoint overlooking Lake Fork Drainage

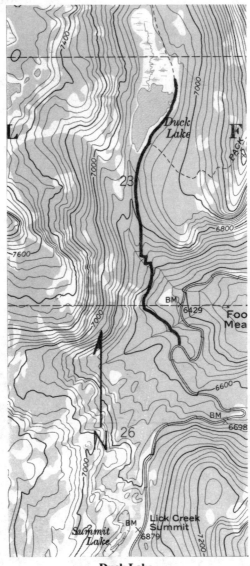

Duck Lake

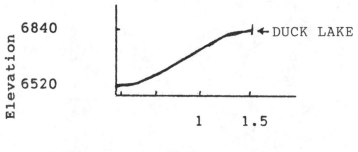

Duck Lake Trail

Duck Lake Trailhead

DUCK LAKE TRAIL
Day hike

Day hike
Distance one direction: 1.5 miles
Elevation gain: 320 feet
Approximate travel time: 1 hour
Topographic map: Box Lake 1969

The trail to Duck Lake is a very easy hike that is well suited for all ages and abilities. An abundance of Bear Grass along the trail blooms in the early spring. At a ½ mile, the trail crosses a small creek, followed by two switchbacks. At 1 mile is the trail to Hum Lake. From this point, it is only a few hundred yards into Duck Lake.

Turn right at McCall Golf Course and follow Lake Shore Drive for 2 miles to Lick Creek Road. Follow Lick Creek Road for 17 miles to Twenty Mile Lakes Trail No. 085, which is on your left (1.5 miles past Lick Creek Summit). Parking is available across the road from the trailhead.

DUCK LAKE LOOKOUT

Newlyweds Eldon and Florence Bruce drifted into McCall and tied their horses to a hitching post along main street. When they walked into the Forestry Office looking for a job, Forest Supervisor Lyle Watts invited them to put in an application for one of two lookout positions that was available. He immediately hired them on the spot.

It was the beginning of summer in 1921 and the annual fire season was still a month away. Their new employer kept them busy threading telephone wire over the mountains towards Yellow Pine. After a dozen or more trips dropping coils of line along the trail, it was time for the couple to gather their supplies and head for Duck Lake Lookout. Following the old blaze trail up Lake Fork Creek, through groves of pine, they came across a hand-hewn log cabin nestled in between a large meadow and a small, glistening lake. Dropping the packs and saddles, Eldon tied bells on the horses and let them roam in the green grass. Florence began sweeping the inside of their new home and was glad to see that no packrats had made the log hut their winter residence. Removing an old pail from the stovepipe, it wasn't long before dinner was ready.

Before sunrise the next morning, the young couple were climbing their way towards the top of a rocky point which would be the official Duck Lake Lookout. From here, they had a bird's-eye view of the surrounding ridges and valleys. The lookout had no house, not even a tent for shelter. Just the clear blue sky overhead and a few weather-beaten pines for shade.

There were very few lookouts back then. One had just been completed at Pilots Peak on the South Fork of the Salmon River. A new two-story log house was on top of Brundage Mountain and on Krassel Knob was another tent.

People and trails were few and far between. One of their closest neighbors was a hermit by the name of "Deadshot" Reed, who squatted on a claim on the South Fork of the Salmon River. By September, ice was beginning to form along the lake's edge. Eldon and Florence climbed up to their lookout for one last time before heading back to McCall for the winter. Duck Lake Lookout was later abandoned in 1923.

Duck Lake

WARREN WAGON ROAD

SECTION 4.

THE DISCOVERY OF GOLD IN WARREN

TWENTY MILE LAKES
Backpack
Mountain bike

THE LEGEND OF POLLY BEMIS

JOSEPHINE LAKE
Day hike

MYSTERY AT LOON LAKE

RUBY MEADOWS TO LOON LAKE LOOP
Mountain bike

LOON LAKE TRAIL
Day hike or backpack
Mountain bike

BURGDORF HOT SPRINGS

Warren, Idaho

THE DISCOVERY OF GOLD
IN WARREN

In 1862, James Warren led a party of prospectors north along the Salmon River into meadows of gold. The word of their discovery quickly spread, and by the following summer the mining camp had grown to over 660 men in search of the rare mineral. From 1869 to 1875, Warren held the county seat. Norman Wiley, a Warren miner, was elected second governor of Idaho. In the fall of 1872, there were only four hundred men in the Warren District. Most of the claims had been worked clean and it did not pay for the "ounce a day" men to continue mining. A vote was taken and the Chinese were allowed to come in. By 1879, 150 whites and 600 Chinese were working in Warren.

Occasionally the Warren Chinese would fight amongst themselves in clans of what was called "Tongs." One "Tong" would war against another, resulting in the bloody death of some of their members. A Chinaman once stole a pair of boots from a white man's house and was thrown in jail. He was told that if he did not return the boots, he would hang. That same day the jailer returned to check on the prisoner and found him down by the creek at the end of a rope.

In 1890, Warren Wagon Road was completed. A wooden steam shovel was introduced in 1904, followed by a pair of electric dredges from 1932 to 1942. The dredge harvest totaled close to 4 million dollars with earlier mining efforts yielding a similar amount.

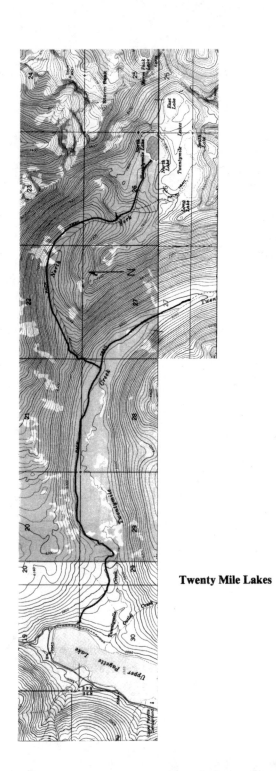

Twenty Mile Lakes

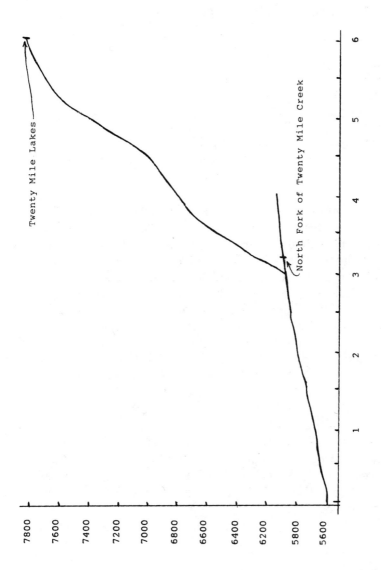

Elevation

7800 7600 7400 7200 7000 6800 6600 6400 6200 5800 5600

Twenty Mile Lakes

North Fork of Twenty Mile Creek

Twenty Mile Lakes: One day trip or backpack; Mountain bike.

TWENTY MILE LAKES TRAIL
Backpack
Mountain bike

Backpack
Distance one direction: 6 miles
Elevation gain: 1,800 feet
Approximate travel time: 4 hours, 30 minutes
Topographic map: U.S.G.S. Black Tip 1963
                          Victor Peak 1969
                          Box Lake 1969

It is not uncommon to see deer and elk along Twenty Mile Lakes Trail. Because of the difficulty in the last 3 miles, it is recommended to spend the night at one of the four pristine high mountain lakes where the fishing is usually excellent.

Follow Warren Wagon Road for 16 miles, a ½ mile past Upper Payette Lake on the right will be Twenty Mile Lakes trailhead with parking and a restroom. The closest drinking water is available back at Upper Payette Lakes Campground. The trail follows Twenty Mile Creek for 3 miles before forking off to the left. In the next ¾ of a mile, the trail is steep with switchbacks. As the grade lessens, you will cross several small creeks and meadows full of wildflowers and beargrass. The last ½ mile is again steep as you hike into a glacially-formed basin.

The first lake you reach is North Lake; a trail to the left takes you through a small saddle and into East Lake. To the right over a small ridge is Long Lake, just east of Long Lake is South Lake. There are several campsites around the lakes to choose from.

TWENTY MILE LAKES TRAIL
Mountain bike
Distance one direction: 4 miles
Elevation gain: 250 feet
Topographic map: U.S.G.S. Black Tip 1963
Victor Peak 1969
Box Lake 1969

For a short, easy ride, the first 3 miles of Twenty Mile Lakes Trail is ideal. The trail has little elevation gain as it crosses several small meadows and creeks. If wanting to continue on to Twenty Mile Lakes, it is best to lock them in a safe place at 3 miles, since the trail does get steep and rocky. For a continued ride, cross the North Fork of Twenty Mile Creek, following the trail as it winds its way towards Duck Lake.

THE LEGEND OF POLLY BEMIS

Born September 11, 1853, to a Chinese peasant family, was a young girl by the name of Lalu Nathoy. Her father, a farmer, lived on one of the upper rivers in China, which was suffering from drought at the time. To prevent the rest of the family from starving, he sold her to a band of outlaws for seed to plant next year's crop. They in turn sold her as a slave girl.

Traveling by ship from San Francisco, an old Chinese woman smuggled her into Portland and sold her for $2,500.00 to a saloon owner by the name of Hong King. On July 8, 1872, at the age of 19, she came to Warren on the back of a horse and was introduced as Polly. She worked in the saloon of her master until a gambler and saloon owner by the name of Charlie Bemis was playing cards late one night with Hong King. At stake was Charlie's money and his saloon; for the Chinaman, it was his slave girl and a little bit of gold. Early the following morning, Charlie walked away with the gold and a Chinese servant.

First as a dance hall hostess and later as a homesteader down on the Salmon River, Polly soon became a friend of lonely Idaho miners. When things would get too rough for five-foot Polly, she would run next door and summon help from Charlie. His quiet and stern personality, along with a reputation for being able to keep a can rolling with a six shooter, saved Polly from many life-threatening situations.

In 1890, a dispute over a poker game left Bemis with a bullet lodged in his left cheek, narrowly missing his eye. A doctor was called in, but could not do much for the ailing gambler. With her crochet hook, Polly cleaned and cared for the wound in her own special way until he recovered.

On August 13, 1894, Charlie decided to marry Polly, since she had saved his life. After the marriage, Bemis bought 15 acres along the Salmon River. Under Polly's care, they raised many fruits and vegetables, along with chickens, ducks and a cow. Two years later, at the age of 47, she received her certificate of residence as a U.S. citizen.

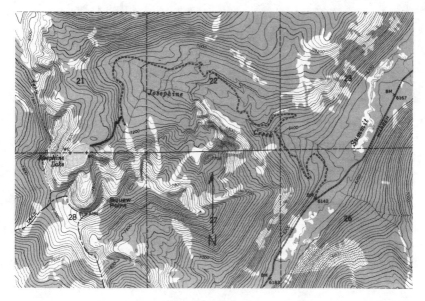

Josephine Lake

JOSEPHINE LAKE
Day hike

Day hike
Distance one direction: ½ mile
Approximate travel time: 30 minutes
Elevation gain: 280 feet
Topographic map: Victor Peak 1969

Josephine Lake Trail is a short, easy hike which is ideal for small children. Granite cliffs enshrine the lake with a waterfall along the west bank. Cold springs feed the emerald waters, providing a natural habitat for trout.

Take Warren Wagon Road for 19.5 miles (2 miles past Secesh Summit) to a road and sign on the left. From here it is 3 miles to Josephine Lake Trail. At the end of the rough and rocky road is the trailhead on the right.

MYSTERY AT LOON LAKE

On January 29, 1943, an Army Airforce B-23 belly-landed on a frozen lake in the center of Idaho's Primitive Area with eight crewmen on board. The B-23 was one of 38 in existence that never saw wartime action. More advanced aircraft such as the B-17 and B-24 had already outdated the bomber. Unique in design because of the rear tailgunner, it was in use on a training flight from Tonopah, Nevada, to McChord Field in Washington.

The plane and crew flew into a major snowstorm outside of Pendleton, Oregon, and lost all radio contact. Being unable to maintain altitude, the plane's radio receiver picked up a Boise radio station while trying to land in Burns, Oregon. As they tried to reach Boise, their radio failed them again. Heavy icing on the wings was causing the plane to lose altitude rapidly and preparations were being made to jump. But just before the order to parachute was given, a glory hole in the clouds enabled the pilot a view of a large, barren, snow-covered opening. Low on fuel and lost, the pilot decided to set down on the frozen surface. Trying to keep the aircraft under control, it was determined that the flaps were frozen in place and couldn't be extended. Circling back around the tree tops, the pilot went in for a second attempt. With the engines off and darkness quickly approaching, he glided onto the frozen lake, sliding across the snow and ice into a thick stand of timber. When the aircraft came to a halt, both wings had been severed at the fuselage and Sergeant Forest B. Hoover had a broken leg.

For five days they waited to be rescued, using the machine guns to cut firewood and the plane as shelter. On February 3, three of the eight men left Loon Lake to find help. Equipped with a shotgun and several chocolate candy bars, they followed the narrows of the Secesh River downstream, searching for a way out of the mountains back to civilization, at times crawling on their hands and knees.

The first day, the three crewmen (ages 19, 24, and 28) walked for 20 hours through waist-deep snow, covering only

44

2 miles. Exhausted by their efforts, they decided to pace themselves, walking for eight hours a day. Several times they had trouble lighting a fire because of blowing snow and an intense, chilling wind. One night the howling of wolves could be heard in the distance; huddled in the frozen darkness they prayed as the sounds grew closer and closer. With only enough rations for one day, they subsisted on stewed chickadees and squirrels. After trudging through waist-deep snow for eight days they came across a cabin (from the Secesh River to the cabin was 10 miles). Finding flour and an old map of the area, the three men rested a day, eating watered down flap-jacks. The map showed a trail leading to McCall over the 6,700-foot Lick Creek Summit, a distance of 32 miles. Once again they started out in search of help. By this time Staff Sergeant Ralph Pruit was having trouble walking. His boots were badly torn and his feet showed signs of severe frostbite. At an abandoned Civilian Conservation Corps camp, the decision was made to leave Sergeant Pruit while the two remaining airmen continued on. Reaching Lake Fork Guard Station, they found a cellar full of food and some flour. Unable to open the locked door, they lit a fire and ate more flapjacks.

Meanwhile, back country bush pilot, Penn Stohr, was on a routine flight to Warren carrying mail and supplies when he spotted several men signaling from the wreckage of the B-23. Unable to land at the time, he flew back to Cascade and reported to Gowen Field in Boise that a two-motor bomber had been spotted on a frozen lake north of McCall. Wanting to fly back that same day and drop supplies to the survivors, he was told by an Army Airforce officer to wait.

The following morning, Penn guided the Airforce to the crash site, where a food drop was made. They overshot their mark and the parachute with the much-needed supplies landed in the trees. While bureaucratic red tape was unwinding, trying to decide what to do next, Penn Stohr flew his "flying cabin on skis" back to Loon Lake and made two hazardous landings bringing the starving airmen back to safety.

A search party of six experienced mountaineers was formed in McCall. Four started at Loon Lake on snowshoes while Warren Brown and Tom Coski started at Krassel Ranger Station also on webs. The two men followed their trail up Lick Creek Summit, sometimes covering the same distance in one hour that it took the three airmen one day to travel. A second plane flown by Bob Fog dropped a note to the two searchers stating that the remaining crewmen had been found.

At the Ranger's District Office in McCall, the surprised operator answered a call from Lake Fork Guard Station, which was closed for the winter. Two of the three missing airmen said that they were safe, but one of their companions had badly frozen feet. Soon afterward, a West Coast Power Company "snow cat" was sent out, pulling a covered sled and toboggan. Rescuers could make it only part way before continuing on snowshoes. At Lake Fork Guard Station, the door was unlocked to the cellar and the two tired airmen feasted on canned grapefruit and corned

Rescue team from McCall. From left to right: Yale Mitchel, Lenord Leitske, Don Parks, Kenny Thomas, Scotty Heater, Gil McCoy, Sargeant Ralph Pruitt in sled.

beef while searchers persevered for six more miles to where Sergeant Pruit lay waiting. Arriving in McCall the next day, they received hot baths at the Hotel McCall and a long anticipated "steak and fries" before returning to Gowen Field in Boise by ambulance.

Three weeks later, "Miracle Pilot" Penn Stohr flew back to the crash site with four Forest Service employees and an Army Airforce Warrant Officer. It was too big a risk to set back down on the lake, so they landed at Secesh Meadows and continued for 9 miles by snowshoe. 1,200 lbs. of salvageable parts were carried back out to the waiting plane. It was believed that the top secret Norden Bombsight was also included in the retrieval. Developed by Carl Norden and Theodore Barth, it enabled pinpoint accuracy in bombing raids during WWI and WWII. It consisted of a telescope with cross hairs, a complex calculating machine and gyroscope. To be effective, it required a straight and level approach and a visible target. The Army Airforce never confirmed nor denied that the Norden Bombsight was on board in their follow-up report of the crash.

For eight men who spent 17 days in the Idaho Wilderness, it is an unbelievable story of comradeship, courage and dedication. Sergeant Forest B. Hoover later had to have his leg amputated above the knee. Pilot Robert Orr, whose skilled flying ability during the emergency landing saved the lives of his passengers and crew, was later shot down and killed while on duty in the South Pacific.

"Miracle Pilot" Penn Stohr at the crash site.

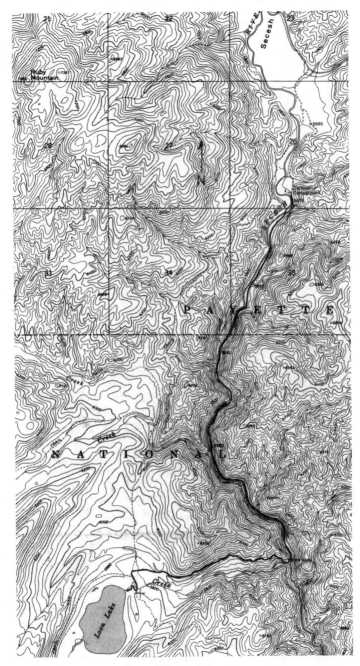

Loon Lake.

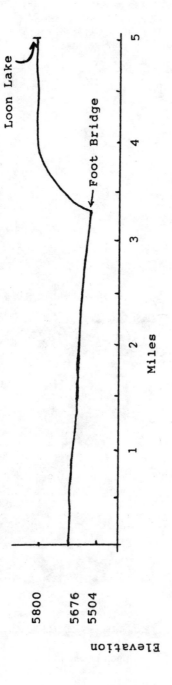

Loon Lake: One day trip or backpack; Mountain bike.

RUBY MEADOWS TO LOON LAKE LOOP
Mountain bike

Mountain bike
Round trip distance: 23 miles
Total variation in elevation: 900 feet
Topographic map: Victor Peak 1969
                     Loon Lake 1969
                     Burgdorf

For those who feel energetic and adventurous, this all day ride offers a variety of terrain and history. Remnants of the early mining and trapping era, along with clear-running creeks and rivers, can be seen. Many of the peaks around Warren and Burgdorf are named after the oldtimers who once mined there. Bear Pete Mountain was named after pioneer Pete Brockenau for the numerous bear stories he loved to tell. Several of the creeks around Ruby Mountain were said to contain precious rubies. Secesh Summit was originally named by southern miners during the war. Secesh Basin was formed centuries ago by glaciers, some of them several miles long.

The Ruby Meadows to Loon Lake Loop ride is steep in places and all sensible safety precautions should be made. Only those in top physical condition should consider this 23-mile loop.

Take Warren Wagon Road north for 22.5 miles. Turn right just before Burgdorf junction onto Ruby Meadows Road. Follow for 1 mile to an old miner's cabin and locked gate. Limited parking space is available here. Just past the gate, the road climbs 200 yards. Continue along the main road, taking the second left to several old mining cabins, past two small ponds, to another larger pond and meadow where four roads intersect. If you missed the mining cabins, you can backtrack down Ruby Creek on the road to your left.

Cross Ruby Creek following the main road around Ruby Meadows for 2 miles to a sign on the left (trail No. 141) to Loon Lake. The trail drops over a ridge into Willow Basket drainage for the next 3 miles. At Victor Creek Trail No. 117, cross over the footbridge and up a ridge overlooking Victor Creek. At the top of the crest, the trail drops back down into a small grass meadow where Loon Lake Trail No. 084 crosses. From the opposite side of the meadow, it is a short ¼ of a mile to Loon Lake.

Return to the large meadow, and instead of taking the Victor Creek Trail, turn right onto Loon Lake Trail. For the next 1.5 miles, the trail drops into the narrows of the Secesh River. Crossing over the river at the footbridge, follow the river upstream for 5 miles to Chinook Campground. One mile past the campground is the main road. Turn left back to Secesh Meadows for 9 miles to Burgdorf Hot Springs where the pavement starts. A ¼ of a mile past this intersection is Ruby Meadows Road.

LOON LAKE
Day hike or backpack
Mountain bike

Day hike or backpack
Distance one direction: 5 miles
Elevation gain: 340 feet
Elevation loss: 172 feet
Approximate travel time: 3 hours
Topographic map: U.S.G.S. Loon Lake 1969
Photoinspected 1979

The first 3.5 miles of the trail to Loon Lake follows the clear rolling waters of the Secesh River. During the months of July and August, an abundance of huckleberries can be found along the trail.

Take Warren Wagon Road north from McCall, for approximately 29 miles to the second bridge that crosses the Secesh River. One mile past the bridge, turn right for 1 mile to Chinook Campground. The Secesh River Trail (No. 080) follows the river's edge to a footbridge where trail No. 084 to Loon Lake begins. After crossing the river next to Loon Creek, the trail rises above the canyon through two switchbacks before gradually leveling off into a thick grove of lodgepole pine. At 5 miles you will come to a small meadow where trail No. 117, Victor Creek Trail, intersects on the right. Cross the meadow to trail No. 084 which is the trail to Duck Lake, Lick Creek Road. From here it is a ¼ of a mile into Loon Lake. There are several campsites along the banks of Loon Creek with more remote sites to the right, around the lake.

LOON LAKE
Mountain bike
Distance one direction: 5 miles
Elevation gain: 340 feet
Elevation loss: 172 feet
Topographic map: U.S.G.S. Loon Lake 1969

For mountain bikes, the trail to Loon Lake offers a variety of terrain that challenges the skill and ability of all riders. The first 3.5 miles follows the Secesh River downstream, rising 30 or more feet above the river then dropping down along the water's edge. This part of the trail is narrow with creek crossings and sections of large granite rocks. After crossing the footbridge, the next ¼ of a mile is steep and sandy with two traverses. Past the switchbacks, the trail climbs moderately along the north side of a small meadow. Cross the meadow at Victor Creek Trail and continue over a small crest into Loon Lake.

BURGDORF HOT SPRINGS

Fred Burgdorf was a German immigrant who arrived at the Warren diggings in 1864 from San Francisco. In 1865, he obtained the water rights to the spring as payment on a promissory note. At that time, only a roadhouse and express station was standing. Being from Germany, Fred was familiar with spas and soon opened a twenty-room hotel with several cabins around the hot mineral water. His hospitality and courtesy filled the resort for fifty-eight years.

In 1902, a singer from Denver by the name of Jeanette Foronsard was passing through to Warren.. Fred and Jeanette married that same year and also changed the name from "Resort" to Burgdorf. Jeanette passed away in 1923. Soon afterwards Fred sold the place to Jim Harris and moved to Weiser, Idaho, where he died and was buried in 1929.

BEAR BASIN

SECTION 5.

A. BEAR BASIN TO THORN CREEK FIRE CAMP; CAR SHUTTLE

B. BEAR BASIN TOWARDS BRUNDAGE MOUNTAIN
Mountain bike
Cross-country ski

EARLY HISTORY OF THE LITTLE SKI HILL

THE LITTLE SKI HILL
Cross-country ski

Bear Basin Road; The Little Ski Hill

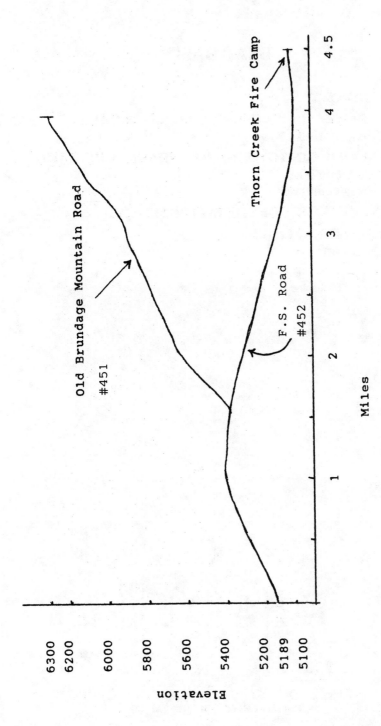

Old Brundage Mountain Road

#451

Thorn Creek Fire Camp

F.S. Road

#452

Elevation

6300
6200
6000
5800
5600
5400
5200
5189
5100

Miles

1   2   3   4   4.5

Bear Basin: Mountain bike; Cross-country ski

BEAR BASIN
Mountain bike
Cross-country ski

A ½ mile west along Highway 55 is Bear Basin Road. This road was originally the only route to Brundage Mountain Lookout. The road gently rolls along for the first 2 miles through large open meadows before dividing into three different directions at the north end of Bear Basin.

A. Bear Basin to Thorn Creek Fire Camp, Car Shuttle
Mountain bike
½ day ride
Distance one direction from Highway 55: 4.5 miles
Elevation gain: 211 feet
Elevation loss: 300 feet
Topographic map: U.S.G.S. Meadows 1973

Take Highway 55 to Brundage Mountain Hazard Lake Road. At ¾ of a mile is the Thorn Creek Fire Camp. On the right is Road No. 452 where one vehicle should be left for the return car shuttle. Beginning back at Bear Basin Road, the first 2 miles roll along through open meadows that blossom with wilflowers from June through August. At the north end of Bear Basin, turn left onto Road No. 452. From here, the road curves and drops for the next 2 miles to Thron Creek Fire Camp. This is a relatively easy ride, since the majority of it is flat through Bear Basin and mostly downhill to Thorn Creek Fire Camp.

B. Bear Basin Towards Brundage Mountain
Mountain bike
½ day ride
Distance one direction: 4 miles
Elevation gain: 1,111 feet
Topographic map: Meadows 1973
                McCall 1973
                Brundage Mountain 1963

From the north end of Bear Basin at the 1.5 mile intersection continue straight to the first fork in the road. Stay right as the road begins to narrow and climb for the next 2 miles. This road does get steep with several viewpoints between three and four miles of Long Valley, Payette Lake and Jughandle Mountain. Many of the other roads in the Bear Basin Area offer an enjoyable afternoon ride with a more moderate climb.

Bear Basin
Cross-country ski

The gentle, rolling slopes of Bear Basin offer a variety of off-track skiing for all abilities and ages. During the winter a car shuttle can also be made from Bear Basin at Highway 55 to Thorn Creek Fire Camp on the Brundage Mountain Road. The tranquil setting along with the sometimes challenging terrain offers the finest in cross-country skiing within a short distance from McCall. For elevations and distances refer to the previous section on mountain bikes at Bear Basin.

EARLY HISTORY OF
THE LITTLE SKI HILL

In 1937, Warren Brown and his father Carl, local logging industrialist, envisioned a community ski hill. A ski hill that would replace the old Blackwell Hill east of McCall where they would walk up to a small jump with a pair of old wooden skis. A suitable parcel of land was donated to the Payette Lakes Ski Club by Brown's Tie and Lumber and was located just 3 miles west of town. As volunteers worked vigorously clearing the way for a ski jump and three runs, millwright Joe Kasper was busy building a toboggan-style sled pulled by a 1,200 foot cable at the saw mill shop in McCall. Fred Williams of the U.S. Forest Service supervised the cutting and hauling of logs from Paddy Flat for a storage shed and day house. The Works Progress Administration and the Civilian Conservation Corps also aided in the on-site construction. Skiing marvel Corey Engen and his brother Alf designed and built the 55-meter jump which would eventually take them and other "jumpers" sailing through the air toward the present-day state highway.

The Little Ski Hill has seen its share of progress and uncertainty throughout the years. In 1953, a T-bar was installed between the jump site and south rim, replacing the old toboggan sled. In 1954, the original log day house was destroyed by fire, along with 200 pairs of skis, boots and poles. Under the leadership of Claude Avery, the community worked together in rebuilding the lodge into its present-day form. In 1968, the Forest Service condemned the old T-bar. Operating with only a temporary rope tow for two years, club members borrowed money from the Farmers Home Administration to buy the lift that is in use today. In 1973, lighting for night skiing was added and the Little Ski Hill hosted the U.S. National Junior Nordic Championships. This was the last time the ski jump has been used. The large wooden structure is now a symbol of The Little Ski Hill's early history when a 200-foot ride down the ramp was what "let's go skiing" was all about.

Preceded only by Sun Valley as the second ski area to be

developed in Idaho, The Little Ski Hill maintains a Non-Profit Organization status. While financial operating costs have risen, ski school rates, season and day passes have remained low so that everyone can participate. Most of the income comes from benefit ski races and fund raising events. When the general economy suffers, so have financial contributions.

In 1944, the "Mighty Mite" program enable the youth of McCall and surrounding communities to train and sharpen their skiing abilities. Twenty-six years of dedication by Ray Watkins, along with other coaches and volunteers, has enable McCall to be represented at many world class skiing events.

The list of Olympic, National and Collegiate skiers who have trained at the hill's 405 vertical feet of alpine slopes, along with over 40 kilometers of groomed nordic ski tracks, is impressive. Corey Engen, Mack Miller, Jean Saubert, Patty Boydstun-Hovedy and Lyle Nelson are just a few to name. Their achievements, along with the many others, is outstanding. Undoubtedly there will be more to come as young skiers begin to train at an early age in the continuing tradition of the Payette Lakes Little Ski Hill.

THE LITTLE SKI HILL
Cross-country ski
40 km of groomed ski trails
Sanctioned biathlon range and marathon courses for racers
Warming hut and day lodge
T-bar lift for telemark and alpine skiers
Track hours are from dusk to dawn
Day and season passes are available

Three miles west of McCall along Highway 55 is The Little Ski Hill. Operated by the Payette Lakes Ski Club, this small ski area is becoming known as one of the finest nordic ski centers in Central Idaho. Over 40 km of well-groomed,, color-coded, nordic ski trails wind through open meadows and timbered ridges. Two km and 5 km sanctioned biathlon courses, a marathon course, skating lanes and telemark

Original Payette Lakes Ski Lodge at The Little Ski Hill

slopes offer a variety of terrain for the novice to advanced skiers. Experienced, qualified instructors have a program for all ages and abilities. Detailed maps of the area can be obtained at either the day lodge or the nordic touring center.

The trails start south of the parking lot (next to the bottom of the T-bar) at the touring center warming hut. A user fee is charged to help cover the cost of trail maintenance.

During the course of the ski season, The Little Ski Hill is the site of several cross-country ski races. One that is increasing in popularity is the Payette Lakes Ski Marathon. The 50 km race is part of the U.S. West Communications Series and is hosted by the Payette Lakes Ski Club and the McCall Memorial Hospital. Skiers can enter the 12K, 25K, or 50K race, which includes a dinner, on-snow race clinics, an awards ceremony and much more. The annual race is scheduled for the last week in January when weather and snow conditions are usually the best. Due to the continuing

success of this race, preregistration is recommended.
   For more information contact:
      The Little Ski Hill
      P.O. Box 442
      McCall, Idaho 83638
      (208) 634-5691

McCall—South Fork Road

HAZARD LAKE ROAD

SECTION 6.

GOOSE CREEK FALLS
Day hike

TWIN LAKES: GRANITE MOUNTAIN
Day hike

GRASS MOUNTAIN LAKES
Day hike or backpack
Mountain bike

UPPER HAZARD LAKE FROM HAZARD LAKE CAMPGROUND
Day hike or backpack
Mountain bike

UPPER HAZARD LAKE FROM HARD CREEK GUARD STATION
Day hike or backpack

LAVA BUTTE LAKES
Day hike or backpack

LAVA RIDGE TRAIL
Day hike or backpack

CLAYBURN TRAIL
Day hike or backpack

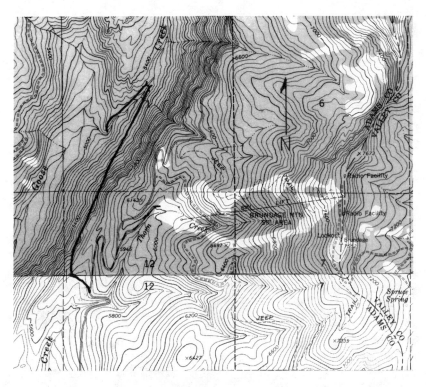

Goose Creek Falls

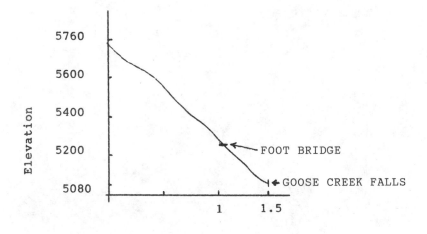

Elevation

5760
5600
5400
5200 ← FOOT BRIDGE
5080 ← GOOSE CREEK FALLS

1   1.5

Miles

Goose Creek Falls: One day trip.

Goose Creek Trail

66

GOOSE CREEK FALLS
Day hike
Distance one direction: 1.5 miles
Elevation loss: 680 feet
Approximate travel time: 1 hour
Topographic map: Brundage Mountain 1963*
                            Meadows 1973*

*Trail is not shown on topographic maps.

Goose Creek Falls from Brundage Mountain, Hazard Lake Road is a relatively easy one and a half mile hike, although to reach the bottom of the falls itself can be difficult for small children.

Take Highway 55 west of McCall, past the Little Ski Hill to Brundage Mountain, Hazard Lake Road. From Highway 55, it is 3 miles to Power Line Trail. Follow this trail west

Foot bridge over Goose Creek

Goose Creek Falls

for 100 yards. At the fork in the trail, stay right, leaving the power line, and continue through a series of gates to a clear cut. The trail rises over a small ridge to a view of Goose Creek Canyon. In the next half mile, you drop several hundred feet to a footbridge that crosses over Goose Creek. Follow the creek downstream for 300 yards. From here there is no marked trail. Continue along the creek to a rocky point; climbing down to the water's edge, you can look back upstream at the cascading waterfall.

There is an old, overgrown trail to Goose Creek Falls from Last Chance Campground. This is not a recommended route due to the difficulty of crossing the creek in the early spring and summer.

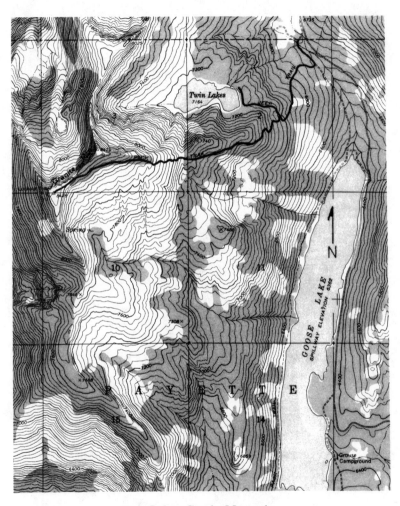

Twin Lakes; Granite Mountain

69

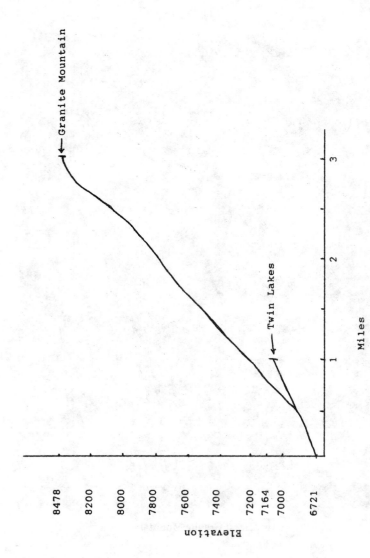

Twin Lakes; Granite Mountain: One day trip.

TWIN LAKES: GRANITE MOUNTAIN

Twin Lakes
Day hike
Distance one direction: 1 mile
Elevation gain: 445 feet
Approximate travel time: 1 hour
Topographic map: Brundage Mountain 1963

Twin Lakes is a reservoir and is best hiked into during the early spring when the lake is full. The trail varies from the 1963 topographic map and now closely follows the old jeep trail. In one mile, the trail climbs along the side of Granite Mountain to a small basin where two lakes form during the fall. Drinking water is available at Grouse Campground on the south end of Goose Lake.

Take Brundage Mountain, Hazard Lake Road (5 miles west of McCall) for 13 miles, (2 miles past Grouse Campground at Goose Lake) and turn left at a large meadow. Just before reaching the Cattlemen's Association stock corrals is the trail to Twin Lakes and Granite Mountain.

Granite Mountain
Day hike
Distance one direction: 3 miles
Elevation gain: 1,758 feet
Approximate travel time: 2 hours
Topographic map: Brundage Mountain 1963

The trail to Granite Mountain is steep and rocky but the view is spectacular. To the south is Cascade Reservoir. To the west are the Wallowa Mountains. To the north is the Little Salmon River Basin and to the east are the Central Idaho Mountains.

A ½ mile up the old jeep trail to Twin Lakes, at the first curve in the road, is a trail to the left. Rock pillars guide the way along a ridge to the summit of Granite Mountain. A manned lookout at the top watches over the region for wildfires.

Upper Hazard Lake
  A. From Hazard Lake Campground
  B. From Hard Creek Guard Station

Grass Mountain Lakes

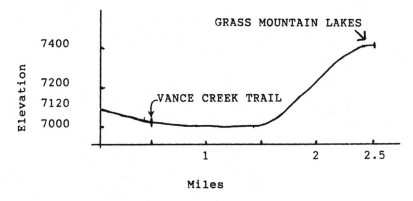

Grass Mountain Lakes: One day trip or backpack.

GRASS MOUNTAIN LAKES
Day hike or backpack
Distance one direction: 2.5 miles
Approximate travel time: 1 hour, 30 minutes
Elevation gain: 400 feet
Topographic map: Hazard Lake 1963

The trail to Grass Mountain Lakes, also called Grassy Twin Lakes, rises uphill through several alpine meadows that offer a picturesque view of glacier-carved granite ridges and Bruin Mountain. Wildflowers embellish the trail from the end of June to the beginning of August.

Grassy Mountain Trail No. 163 is the first of two trailheads that lead to Grassy Twin Lakes and is approximately 5 miles past Goose Lake on your left. Parking is only available for a few cars. A ½ mile further up the road (18 miles from Highway 55) is Hard Creek Guard Station with ample parking. Vance Creek Trail intersects with Grassy Mountain Trail at .5 of a mile. Take the trail to the left at this intersection and climb steadily through an open slope, dipping down into a small forest, then back up into a large meadow. The first of Grass Mountain Lakes is to the left. A ¼ of a mile further up the trail is the upper lake, which is deeper and has several campsites to choose from.

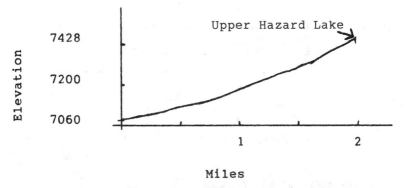

Upper Hazard Lake from Hazard Lake Campground: One day trip or backpack; Mountain bike.

UPPER HAZARD LAKE
A. From Hazard Lake Campground
B. From Hard Creek Guard Station

A. Upper Hazard Lake From Hazard Lake Campground
Day hike or backpack
Mountain bike
Distance one direction: 2 miles
Elevation gain 368 feet
Approximate travel time: 1 hour
Topographic map: U.S.G.S. Hazard Lake 1963

Take Highway 55 west of McCall for 5 miles to Brundage Mountain Ski Area, Hazard Lake Road. From Highway 55, it is 22 miles to the trailhead at Hazard Lake Campground, where drinking water is also available. The pavement ends in 4 miles at the ski area. A well-graveled road winds its way past a scenic viewpoint of Goose Creek and New Meadows.

At the campground, the trail starts at two different locations within 100 yards of each other. One starts at campsite No. 5 in the campground. The other trailhead has parking and is south of the entrance. Both intersect each other in a short distance.

The first mile of Upper Hazard Lake Trail is flat. Mountain bicyclists will find this section of the trail bumpy from tree roots that criss-cross the path in several places. The trail follows the edge of two large meadows before climbing a ¼ of a mile through a garden of rocks into Upper Hazard Lake.

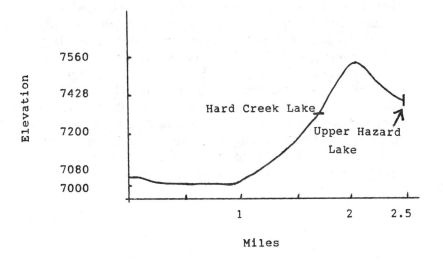

Upper Hazard Lake from Hard Creek Guard Station: One day trip or backpack.

B. Upper Hazard Lake from Hard Creek Guard Station
Day hike or backpack
Distance one direction: 2.5 miles
Approximate travel time: 1 hour, 30 minutes
Elevation gain: 560 feet
Elevation loss: 212 feet
Topographic map: Hazard Lake 1963

Take Highway 55, 5 miles west of McCall to the Brundage Mountain Ski Area, Hazard Lake Road. Follow this road for 18 miles to Hard Creek Guard Station (5.5 miles past Goose Lake). The trailhead is located at the east end of a large meadow on the right, across from Grass Mountain Lakes Trail. parking, campsites, and a toilet are also situated here. Drinking water can be obtained from Hazard Lake Campground, 2 miles to the north. This trail is not recommended for mountain bikes due to the large ruts, steepness, and rocks. The first mile adheres to the side of several grass slopes overlooking Hard Creek drainage. Stay left at an unmarked fork in the trail. This section of the trail into Upper Hazard lake is not shown on the topographic map. Continue through large granite boulders in between a forest of spruce and fir to Hard Creek Lake. The trail follows the right side of the lake, over a small saddle into granite-shrouded Upper Hazard Lake.

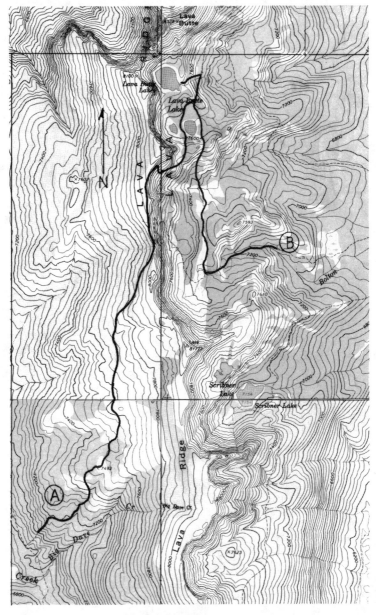

Lava Butte Lakes
A. Lava Ridge Trail
B. Clayburn Trail

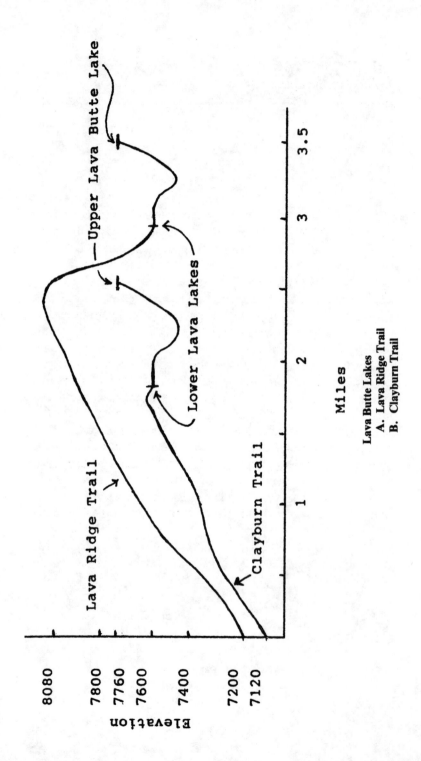

Elevation

8080
7800
7760
7600
7400
7200
7120

Miles

1   2   3   3.5

Lava Ridge Trail

Clayburn Trail

Upper Lava Butte Lake

Lower Lava Lakes

Lava Butte Lakes
A. Lava Ridge Trail
B. Clayburn Trail

A. LAVA BUTTE LAKES, LAVA RIDGE TRAIL
Day hike or backpack
Distance one direction: 3.5 miles
Elevation gain: 1.040 feet
Elevation loss: 480 feet
Approximate travel time: 2 hours
Topographic map: U.S.G.S. Hershey Point 1963
Patrick Butte 1964

Take Highway 55, 5 miles west of McCall to Brundage Mountain Ski Area, Hazard Lake Road. Follow this road for 25 miles (3 miles past Hazard Lake Campground) to Elk Meadows Road No. 308. Elk Meadows Road is not charted on the topographic maps, but is shown on the Payette Lakes Visitors Map. A ½ mile on Elk Meadows Road, on the left is Lava Ridge Trail next to Big Dave Creek. From here it is 3.5 miles to Lava Lakes, 4 miles to Elk Meadows Road and 8 miles to Hershey Point Lookout.

This trail is one of the highest in the Payette National Forest, offering a panoramic view of the surrounding valleys and mountains. The first ½ mile readily ascends onto Lava Ridge. Through open grassy slopes, the trail winds along overlooking Elk Meadows to the east, Hard Butte, Patrick Butte and the Seven Devils to the west. At 2 miles, a trail crosses from Lava Lakes. This can be used as a loop trail on the return hike. Follow the ridge for another ¼ of a mile to where the trail descends over the side of Lava Ridge and into Lava Lakes, converging with Clayburn Trail. A ¼ of a mile further to the north, over a small rise, is a creek coming from Upper Lava Lake. Twenty-five yards to the north on the left is an unmarked trail that climbs up the side of a hill and into Upper Lava Lake.

B. LAVA BUTTE LAKES, CLAYBURN TRAIL

Day hike or backpack
Distance one direction: 2.5 miles
Elevation gain: 640 feet
Approximate travel time: 1 hour, 30 minutes
Topographic map: U.S.G.S. Hershey Point 1963
Patrick Butte 1964

Take Highway 55, 5 miles west of McCall to Brundage
Mountain Ski Area, Hazard Lake Road. Follow this road
for 25 miles (3 miles past Hazard Lake Campground) to Elk
Meadows Road No. 308. Elk Meadows Road is not charted
on the topographic maps but is shown on the Payette Lakes
Visitors Map, which can be obtained at the Payette National
Forest, Rangers Headquarters Office in McCall. Continue
on Elk Meadows Road for 8 miles to Clayburn Trail on the
left. Hazard Lake Campground has the closest available
drinking water.

The trail begins with a gradual incline for the first ½
mile along Bolton Creek, intersecting at 1 mile with an
unmarked trail from Lava Ridge. Turn right, staying to the
east side of a large meadow, as the trail begins to run
parallel to the rugged volcanic ridge of Lava Butte. Rising
through a small crest in the trail, Lower Lava Lake can be
seen. Still hidden in a pocket of volcanic cliffs and pine trees
is Upper Lava Lake, a little more difficult to find, but
equally as picturesque. Continue past Lower Lava Lake to
where an adjoining trail from Lava Ridge intersects. A ¼
of a mile further down the trail, over a small ridge, is a
creek bed that can be dry in the ending summer months.
Twenty-five yards to the north on the left is an unmarked
trail that climbs up the side of the hill into the turquoise
waters of Upper Lava Lake.

Bibliography

IDAHO FOR THE CURIOUS; Cort Conley, Backeddy Books

IDAHO CHINESE LORE; Sister M. Alfreda Elsensohn, Idaho Corporation of Benedictine Sisters; Cottonwood, Idaho

THE IDAHO STORY Vol. II; Idaho Poets and Writers Guide, Ipas Publishing Co.

PIONEER DAYS IN IDAHO COUNTY Vol. II; Sister M. Alfreda Elsensohn, Caxton Printers Ltd.

FIRE LOOKOUTS OF THE NORTHWEST; Ray Kresek, Ye Gallon Press; Fairfield, Washington

THE STORY OF MY LIFE; By Helen Keller, Grosset and Dunlap Publishers, New York

Acknowledgements

Ray and Harriet Jorgenson
Mark and Judy Larson
Warren and Jane Brown
John Shaw
Leonard and Judy Williams
Irene Vance
John and Virginia Boydstun
Ned Jackson
Jack Kappas
The Boise Public Library
The Central Idaho Star News
The McCall Public Library

A special thank you to family and friends who knowingly or unknowingly contributed in some way, a part of themselves into the preceding pages.